ELIZABETH RING

PATROL DOGS

KEEPING THE PEACE

GOOD DOGS!
THE MILLBROOK PRESS · BROOKFIELD, CONNECTICUT

FOR MIMI AND NANAOO,
SUPER PEACEKEEPERS

The author wishes to thank Sgt. David Barger and
his staff at the Connecticut State Police K-9
Training Center for their goodwill in going above
and beyond the call of duty to assist in the
preparation of *Patrol Dogs* and *Detector Dogs*.

Cover photo courtesy of Bill Hennefrund
Photos courtesy of Bill Hennefrund: pp. 3, 4, 14, 16,
19, 21, 23; Sgt. Walter Clark: p. 7; UPI/Bettmann:
pp. 9, 17; Wide World Photos: pp. 10, 27; Reuters/
Bettmann: p. 12; Sgt. Malcolm Deuser: p. 24.

Library of Congress Cataloging-in-Publication Data

Ring, Elizabeth, 1920-
Patrol dogs : keeping the peace / by Elizabeth Ring.
p.   cm. — (Good dogs!)
Includes bibliographical references and index.
Summary: Reveals how K-9 teams work and how
dogs are selected and trained to perform police work.
ISBN 1-56294-291-3 (lib. bdg.)
1. Police dogs—United States—Juvenile literature.
[1. Police dogs.]   I. Title.   II. Series.
HV8025.R57   1994
636.7'0886—dc20   93-15662 CIP AC

Published by The Millbrook Press
2 Old New Milford Road
Brookfield, Connecticut 06804

SAINT MARY'S SCHOOL
309 E. Chestnut Street
Lancaster, Ohio 43130

PATROL DOGS

Intelligence shines in the eyes of this German shepherd. Among all the breeds used for police work, the German shepherd stands out for its agility, fearlessness, and obedience.

In Greenwood Village, Colorado, one March afternoon, a drug-crazed woman staggered around in the middle of a busy street, waving a pistol at everyone in sight.

The Arapahoe County police arrived, but they could not get near the lady with the gun.

"I'll shoot!" she screamed, aiming the gun every time an officer made a move.

The police had no wish for a gun battle. They wanted nobody killed. So, using a bullhorn, they spent an hour and a half trying to talk her into surrendering. It was no use.

As her threats grew wilder, the police finally had to ask Corporal Walter Clark of the Greenwood Village police force to send in his black-and-tan German shepherd dog, Rondo, to disarm the woman.

When she saw Rondo, the woman screamed: "If you turn that dog loose I'll shoot him!"

Corporal Clark knew the risk he was asking Rondo to take. But he also knew that it would be hard for the unsteady woman to take aim on a fast-moving target like a dog.

At Corporal Clark's command, "bise!" (meaning "bite" in Germany, where the dog had been born and raised), Rondo took off—a bundle of speed, muscle, and well-trained know-how.

A shot rang out, then another, and another. Rondo staggered and almost fell, but he did not stop. He lunged for the woman's arm, catching it just above her hand. His grip knocked the gun from her hand as she fell to the ground.

Immediately, the police moved in. Corporal Clark called Rondo off and, with the help of a fellow officer, bound up the dog's bleeding foot. Other officers arrested the woman, who was taken to a medical center to be treated for her bite wounds.

Rondo's left front foot was shattered. Yet in just a few days, the dog was back at work with a cast on his leg. Rondo was hailed as a hero and became the first dog in Colorado to earn a Medal of Valor.

Later, when Rondo's foot had healed, he and Corporal Clark (who later was promoted to Sergeant) were invited to visit many schools. Children always had a lot of questions to ask about Rondo, the hero of Arapahoe County.

"Yes," Corporal Clark would answer the question most often asked, "Rondo *is* a very brave dog." He told about other times when Rondo had acted fearlessly on patrol—like the time he pulled down a burglar armed with a knife.

And to another question often asked, he would answer, "Yes, Rondo did bite the woman, but no, he is not a mean, vicious dog. You notice that Rondo grabbed the woman's arm. That made her drop her gun. Rondo would not go for anyone's throat, and he would not bite as hard as he could. If he wanted to, he could put about seven hundred and fifty pounds of pressure into his bite. A person's hardest bite is no more than sixty pounds."

Then Corporal Clark would explain how Rondo had been carefully trained to bite just hard enough to hold a person. "Most important," he would say, "he is trained to let go on command.

Corporal Walter Clark and his K-9 partner, Rondo. Rondo
was awarded Colorado's Medal of Valor for his bravery during
an attack that left him seriously wounded.

He's not going to kill anyone. Except when he is *commanded* to attack, Rondo is as friendly as a dog can be."

Corporal Clark always invited the children to pet the dog, whose wagging tail, wet tongue, and warm brown eyes showed just how delighted he was with their attention.

DOGS IN POLICE SERVICE · Rondo is typical of most dogs in police patrol service. He is a male German shepherd trained to be a canine (dog) partner to a police officer in a K-9 (short for "canine") team.

German shepherd dogs were first used in police work in Germany. The dogs had been bred and trained in that country for many years to herd and protect flocks of cattle and sheep. Police dogs guard and protect people instead of animals.

The dogs' instinct to guard and guide, most animal scientists believe, probably goes back to their ancestors. When wild dogs travel in groups, for instance, strong male dogs often trot on the edge of the group, protecting the less strong dogs in the center of the pack.

New York City was, in 1907, the first American city to use dogs in police work. But it was not until the 1950s that big police K-9 programs were started. Today there are police K-9 corps in hundreds of towns and cities all over the United States.

DUTIES OF A POLICE K-9 TEAM · On duty, a police patrol K-9 team has many jobs. Together the dog and its partner tour an area, either on foot or in a car. The dog wears a tag or collar that identifies it as a member of the police force.

Even before official K-9 programs were started, New York City policemen used dogs to fight crime. This photo, taken in 1943, shows officers setting out with their muzzled partners to patrol the streets.

When the police work gets especially dangerous, some patrolmen make sure that their dogs wear bulletproof vests.

Since their chief job is helping to keep the peace and protect the public, the partners are constantly on the lookout for threatening activity, such as a prowler at a window or a mugger on the street. They are also on call from other officers who need the help of a K-9 team.

The K-9 team patrols streets, alleys, yards, buildings. The dog (with its keen sense of hearing as well as smell) may warn its partner—by cocking its ears, breaking its stride, stopping, or giving a low growl—of dangers that the partner might not hear or see. The dog will risk its own life to attack (without any command) anyone who threatens its partner.

Sometimes, by just looking powerful, the dog assists in controlling crowds or in making a criminal think twice before committing a crime. On command, the dog searches for people who are lost or who might be hiding. Whether on leash or off, the dog is always alert to its partner's next command.

The dog also searches for items such as stolen property or, perhaps, a gun dropped by a suspect. It chases suspects who try to run away or who refuse to come out of a place when ordered. And (like Rondo) it attacks on command and holds a suspect until its partner tells it to let go.

WHAT IT TAKES TO BE A POLICE SERVICE DOG · German shepherds are powerful dogs. Bred to be work dogs, they are strong and hardy. Their dense coats are weatherproof in wind, rain, snow, and sleet. They can travel long distances and work long hours without tiring. They have a keen sense of smell. They are very bright, alert dogs that learn easily and seem to enjoy their work.

For patrol duty, police departments generally favor males over females. Males are larger than females and usually more aggressive. That is, they are more willing to attack when they are ordered to.

While German shepherds are considered the best all-around police dog, they are not the only breed in police work. For

Members of the New York police K-9 unit outside the World Trade Center after a bomb went off there in 1993. The dogs were waiting to be sent into the building to search for bodies.

instance, Labrador retrievers and golden retrievers (plus a few other breeds) make great detector dogs. These "D-dogs," as they are sometimes called, are specialists. They are trained to sniff out narcotics and bombs. They are taught to detect accelerants (such as gasoline, kerosene, and other fire-starters) used by arsonists to start unlawful fires. And they are trained to find bodies of victims buried in the rubble of earthquakes, hurricanes, and other disasters. Male and female dogs work at these jobs that require intelligence, a gentle disposition, and a well-trained sniffing ability.

Bloodhounds are specialists, too. They can be trained to be expert trackers. Like German shepherds, they are tireless trailers of people, whether crime suspects or people who are lost, hidden, buried, or dead. However, unlike the all-purpose German shepherds, bloodhounds are not skilled in other police work.

Other kinds of dogs that make good canine cops include Doberman pinschers, rottweilers, boxers, Airedales, giant schnauzers, Belgian Malinois, and some other smart, hardy breeds.

Although some dogs in United States police service are bought from breeders, most are donated. New dogs (usually obtained when they are between twelve and sixteen months old) are checked out in several ways. Previous owners fill out forms that describe the dogs' temperament (personality), habits, and training. Veterinarians examine them to make sure they are healthy. Trainers work with them to test their abilities.

WHAT IT TAKES TO BE A POLICE DOG'S PARTNER · At police K-9 training centers in the United States, both dogs and their partners spend about three months learning to work together. Dogs and officers are carefully matched. Unless they get along really well, they cannot make a good working team. Their lives may someday depend on their loyalty to each other.

Police officers volunteer for K-9 duty. The men and women who apply are checked out as thoroughly as the dogs. In most training centers, officers must have been in the police force for at least two years to qualify as K-9 partners. They must be in excellent physical condition. They must be patient, dependable, even-tempered people who are committed to police work in general. They must, of course, like dogs—and so must their families, since most police service dogs live at home with their partners.

Patrol dogs are more than a trooper's partner—they are part of a trooper's family. The dogs shown here have a happy home life, filled with backyard games and lots of loving attention.

TRAINING: BASIC OBEDIENCE · One day, a police K-9 corps officer and his dog, Randy, were patrolling a city street. The trooper saw a man grab a pocketbook from a woman and run. When the man did not stop when ordered to, the trooper let his dog off leash and commanded, "Get him!"

The dog raced off after the purse-snatcher.

Just then, the trooper noticed that the robber was running straight toward a plainclothes officer. That officer, the trooper could see, was ready to stop the man.

To call off the dog, the trooper yelled, "Randy, out! Heel!"

Immediately, the dog halted, swung around, and trotted back to the trooper.

"Good boy, Randy," the trooper said.

To make sure a dog will obey as promptly as Randy did takes weeks of hard training—for both the dog and its partner. Training of K-9 teams begins with classes in basic obedience. The partners (perhaps having met for the first time at the first training class) get acquainted. Maybe they go jogging together or play "fetch" with sticks and tennis balls. During this time, the two bond, forming a close friendship that neither will ever want to break.

Even when the team knuckles down to business, each exercise is another "game." A key part of training is making sure that the dogs enjoy their work. As days go by, the officers learn how to get the dogs to obey willingly, and the dogs become quicker and more expert in responding to commands such as "sit," "down," "stay," "come," "heel," and "no."

The dogs learn to respond to both voice and hand signals. Hand signals are especially important, because there are times (such as in a search for a suspect in hiding) when the partners have to work very quietly. So, for example, at the same time the "heel" command is given, the officer slaps his left leg with his left hand. The hand command for "sit" is raising a right hand, palm up; the signal for "down" is lowering a hand, palm down.

K-9 patrol troopers take their partners through obedience-training class. Instant response to both voice commands and hand signals is demanded.

A group of police dogs in training obey the "stay" command
as a cat strolls by—a major distraction.

When a dog makes a mistake, gets distracted (perhaps by a cat), or chooses not to obey, the partner never punishes the dog by hitting or getting angry. That would only make the dog less willing to obey. However, commands are always firmly given. For instance, if the dog does not "come" on command, the partner might give a hard jerk on the leash or use a sharp tone of voice (but not shout). Sometimes an officer might have to take hold of each side of the dog's neck and give the dog a good shake to point out a repeated fault.

When the dog finally obeys, it gets many pats and much praise. That way, the dog learns that when it obeys instantly, it is instantly rewarded. Unhesitating obedience is absolutely necessary to the success of any police K-9 operation.

TRAINING: AGILITY SKILLS · One night, when a police K-9 team was investigating a robbery, a suspect ran down a dark alley and scrambled over a wall. The K-9 team followed. Just as the dog and its partner dropped to the other side of the wall, the suspect was disappearing through a hole in the fence on the opposite side of the yard.

On the run, the officer unclasped the dog's leash.

"Get him!" he commanded.

The dog plunged through the fence hole and into the next yard. The dog was holding the suspect's leg in his jaws when its partner caught up.

"Out, heel," said the officer. The dog let go of the man's leg, and the officer made the arrest.

Agility training for dogs is something like track-and-field training for people. The dogs, naturally athletic and agile, practice racing, high jumping, long jumping, bounding over hurdles—plus several other exercises.

The training not only keeps the dogs fit, it makes them unafraid to climb ladders, leap over walls or off high ledges, scramble through windows, crawl through pipes and across narrow bridges, beat their way through dense shrubbery, plow through mud, and run alongside ditches to find their way across.

In agility training, patrol dogs learn to climb ladders and walls, jump through windows, scramble through mazes, and do many more things that require great strength and skill.

The energetic dogs seem to love the on-the-job acrobatics that their partners sometimes find hard to master.

TRAINING: ATTACK · While Corporal Clark's partner, Rondo, was learning to attack and hold a person, he went through a rigorous program called "agitation." In this practice, dogs are agitated, or stirred up, to make them excited enough to attack. This is to make the dogs understand that at certain times they must bite—either to protect a partner or to grab a crime suspect. A patrol dog must learn not only to bite and hold a suspect and to let go the minute its partner commands, but it must also learn to attack on its own if its partner is threatened or attacked.

During training, a dog's partner holds the dog on a leash while another trainer yells, growls, waves a stick, and runs toward the dog. The dog tries to leap toward the "threatening" trainer. As soon as the "agitator" backs off, the dog relaxes.

After the exercise is over, the dog is apt to lie down and wag its tail or play with a ball. It is clear that the dog is not really upset or angry and that it sees this teasing play as just another game.

Once the dog has gone through "agitation" training, it learns to attack by first playing a game of tug-of-war. A trainer (again, not the dog's partner), wearing padded sleeves, plays this game with a rag. As the training goes on, one end of the rag is tied to the trainer's arm. The rag is gradually shortened until, when the dog grabs the rag, its teeth get hold of the padded sleeve, and the dog is "attacking."

This patrol dog, hearing the command "Get him!", leaps at the padded arm of a trooper during an attack-training session. The dog is also trained to let go immediately, on the "out, heel" command.

Some dogs refuse to attack. Even though they are fine dogs, they have to be dropped from the patrol-dog course. However, some who fail this part of patrol-dog training go into some other line of duty, such as detector-dog work, and have good, long careers as K-9 specialists.

TRAINING: BUILDING SEARCH · One dark, moonless night, a K-9 police officer received a call to assist two other officers in a search for a crime suspect who had run into a waterfront warehouse.

At the warehouse door, the trooper yelled, "Come out or I'll release my dog."

When there was no action, the trooper said, "Find him," and let the dog off leash.

All three officers stood, alert and listening, just inside the door as the dog searched. Before long, the dog started barking, and the officers ran toward the sound, guns drawn. The dog had stopped by a closet door and in a moment the officers had wrenched the door open and grabbed their suspect, with no shots fired.

Patrol dogs are often called on to search a building, tracking a human scent from floor to floor and through many rooms. The dog is trained for this in an exercise called the "box search." A trainer hides in one of several large crates. The dog's partner gives the command "search" or "find him." He then lets the dog off leash. The dog sniffs the boxes until it locates the human smell. Then it alerts its partner to the hiding place by scratching, biting, or barking.

TRAINING: TRACKING · One cool, foggy day, the police of Jefferson County, Kentucky, had to track down a murder suspect. Sergeant Malcolm Deuser and his sleepy-looking bloodhound,

At the
command
"Find him!",
patrol
dogs use
their eyes,
ears, and
noses to
inspect
buildings
where a
suspected
criminal
may be
hiding.

A. J. (short for Amanda Junior), answered the call. The dog took one sniff of the suspect's cap and set out on a steady run.

Sergeant Deuser hung onto her leash as A. J. pulled hard, following the strong ground scent that led her straight to a railroad track. A. J. followed the trail, her nose to the rail, her long, floppy ears swinging at the sides of her swaying, loose-skinned head.

Sergeant Malcolm Deuser follows his bloodhound A.J. as she puts her nose to the ground to track a criminal.

A. J. was so hot on the trail that Sergeant Deuser had to yank her off the railroad track when a train came along. As soon as the train had passed, the eager dog went right back to sniffing. Within minutes, she made a beeline for the suspect, who had hunched himself into a ball, trying to hide in thick bushes alongside the tracks. Sergeant Deuser took charge, while A. J., her mission completed, wagged her tail twice and lay down, yawning.

Tracking is one of a police service dog's most important jobs. As in other exercises in police K-9 training, bloodhounds and other tracking and detector dogs are taught to find people or objects by playing games.

Each dog's remarkable sense of smell (a million or more times more powerful than a human's) is trained to identify and track the scent of particular substances or persons.

In learning to track, a dog first works with its own partner. The partner throws an object (the partner's shoe, perhaps) and trains the dog to bring it back. Next, after the dog has sniffed the shoe, the partner walks off and drops the shoe a short distance away.

"Find it," the partner says. Or the words may be "seek," "search," "look for it," "track," or even "sook" (which sounds like a German word meaning "seek").

The dog, familiar with its partner's scent, learns to follow the partner's trail that leads to the shoe—first in a straight line, then making turns, then along trails that cross other paths walked by the partner.

122515

Next, the shoe is hidden and the partner and several other people walk around, crossing each other's paths. Since the dog knows its partner's scent well, it ignores the scents of the other people and follows its partner's scent to the shoe.

Later, the dog is taught to follow the scent of another trainer. Finally, the dog learns to follow any person's scent after smelling some item that that person has touched.

Bloodhounds are said to have the keenest sense of smell of all dogs. But a Doberman pinscher named Sauer holds the tracking record. In 1925 this dog trailed a thief for 100 miles (160 kilometers) across South African plains—as hot on the scent as any dog can be.

At the end of their training, dogs are certified as patrol dogs. They are ready to help prevent crime and to enforce laws wherever their partners are called upon to work.

Many police departments report a drop in crime when dogs become part of a police force. Whether the dogs are patrolling in high-crime areas, searching airports, schools, parks, office buildings, chasing suspects through woods, fields, city streets, or merely standing by when a crowd gathers, the dogs do their work well. Their intelligence, courage, agility, and obedience are tested daily.

At most police K-9 training centers, the dogs return once a month to practice their skills—especially in obedience, searching, and tracking.

A motorcycle officer and his canine partner—and passenger.

Later, when they are more experienced on the beat and have proved themselves reliable, they return for about five days each year to review all their skills. At this time they brush up on little-used skills (such as attack, perhaps) or skills that may need improvement. These yearly refresher courses continue until the dogs retire at age ten or twelve, when they trade in their police badges for civilian dog tags.

By the end of their working days, the peacekeepers have earned a good rest, usually as a companion for their partner, who will now train a new, young dog.

"Sometimes," one police officer said of his retired dog, "my old partner whimpers in his sleep. His legs twitch, his nose wrinkles, and his tail thumps the floor. I'll bet anything he's dreaming of being on patrol with me again. He really loved his work."

FURTHER READING

Curtis, Patricia. *Dogs on the Case*. New York: Dutton, 1989.

Davidson, Margaret. *Seven True Dog Stories*. New York: Hastings House, 1982.

Handel, Leo H. *A Dog Named Duke: True Stories of German Shepherd Dogs at Work with the Law*. New York: Lippincott, 1966.

O'Neill, Catherine. *Dogs on Duty*. Washington, D.C.: National Geographic Books, 1988.

Silverstein, Alvin, and Virginia Silverstein. *Dogs, All About Them*. New York: Lothrop, Lee and Shepard, 1986.

INDEX

ABOUT THE AUTHOR

Free-lance writer and editor Elizabeth Ring is a former teacher and an editor at *Ranger Rick's Nature Magazine*. Her previous books for children include two biographies, *Rachel Carson: Caring for the Earth* and *Henry David Thoreau: In Step with Nature*, published by The Millbrook Press. Also published by The Millbrook Press are two other books by Elizabeth Ring in the *Good Dogs!* series, *Detector Dogs: Hot on the Scent* and *Assistance Dogs: In Special Service*. She has also written on a range of programs on environmental subjects for the National Wildlife Federation. She lives in Woodbury, Connecticut, with her husband, writer and photographer William Hennefrund. Although five dogs have been a part of the family over the years, three cats are current companions.